HURRICANE PROTOCOL

Books by House of Nehesi Publishers

Plastered in Pretty
N.C. Marks

Schoolboy in Wartime – Memories of My Early Life
Gerard van Veen

Fantasies – Love-making poems
Fabian Adekunle Badejo

Liviticus
Kamau Brathwaite

Book of the Dead
Lasana Sekou

The Unseen Letter – A Play in Five Acts
Glen C. Nairn

Columbus, the Moor | Colón, el Moro
Colomb, le Maure | Colombo, il Moro
(English, español, français, italiano)
Charles Matz

The Adulterous Citizen – poems stories essays
Tishani Doshi

Language, Culture, and Identity in St. Martin
Rhoda Arrindell

Haiti and Trans-Caribbean Literary Identity
Haití y la transcaribeñidad literaria
Emilio Jorge Rodríguez

Sovereignty of the Imagination
Language and the Politics of Ethnicity
Conversations III
George Lamming

National Symbols of St. Martin – A Primer
Edited by Lasana M. Sekou

Lasana M. Sekou

HURRICANE PROTOCOL

House of Nehesi Publishers
P.O. Box 460
Philipsburg, St. Martin
Caribbean

WWW.HOUSEOFNEHESIPUBLISH.COM
www.facebook.com/nehesipublishers
http://twitter.com/#!/HouseofNehesi

ISBN: 9781733633307

Acknowledgement: This book has been made possible in part through a contribution from the BK Martin Memorial Book Fund.

Cover: Nimojin Media Design. Cover digital art: Sundiata Lake.
Illustrations, from the *Dresden Codex* color reproductions by Lacambalam, 2001 (wikipedia.org/wiki/Maya_codices#/media/File:Láminas_8_y_9_del_Códice_de_Dresden.jpg).
Photography: Saltwater Collection/HNP.

"The gale doesn't stop at the frontier."*

[*Traditional saying about the unity of St. Martin]

Contents

HURRICANE PROTOCOL

[A] Statement[1]

What follows is a selection of "Hurricane Protocol" poems, written with unaccustomed reluctance. They are sketches of observations, memory recovery exchanges about personal, familial, and community experiences during the passing and aftermath of hurricane Irma.

On September 6, 2017, St. Martin was struck by the category 5 hurricane, the most destructive natural disaster recorded for the Caribbean island. About 90% of the island's homes and natural environment was devastated by the storm—dashing electricity and communication lines to the ground; closing water supply; felling trees; ripping roofs from houses, schools, and hotels and other businesses; destroying or disrupting at length all ports; polluting wetlands. For St. Martin's people, the passing of the equally powerful hurricane Maria on September 19 added a heightened sense of terror to the catastrophic "cut-ass&wreckage" (p. 9) from Irma. The overall destruction and recovering "value" is billed in the billions of USA dollars. St. Martin is, historically, since the unholy centuries of Slavery, a nation of one people, but still divided politically. The island's southern half is a territory of the Netherlands; the northern part is a territory of France.

Missing from these poems are more references drawn directly from "local," regional, and international news and social media; from the economic advantage taken by the powerful and the greedy "in this short-/age time of everything that they" too "prey&/pilfer" (p. 17); and from the codes of political procedures and conduct in the colonies and from the countries holding fast to the colonies in miserly fashion and *dis*-function: Dutch, French, British, American. Therein probably lies the persistent feeling of reluctance about these poems that are more about personal, familial, community accounts (new "territories" for me) than the socio-political (a preference).

The eventful Atlantic hurricane season of 2017 garnered global attention. In addition to the "Charismatically Caribbean" St. Martin, the hurricanes, particularly Irma and Maria, affected millions of people and ravaged most of the countries, islands, territories along the region's northeastern/Greater Antilles "arc" (p. 21): Dominica, Guadeloupe, Barbuda, St. Barths, Anguilla, the Virgin Islands, Puerto Rico, Dominican Republic, Haiti, Turks and Caicos, Cuba, The Bahamas …

The images that tenant these poems are of a cyclonic provenance that has generated the loss of human life and ongoing displacement, migration and emigration; destruction to homes and livelihood, to what was already a largely fragile infrastructure; to an even more sensitive domestic food production and practically non-existent reserve; and to a highly stressed natural environment. Many of us are in recovery mode, some too painfully slow, some barely at all, well into 2019 and in certain cases threatening to go beyond. In these poems—reaching out of trauma, hopefully with healing substance, hollering from St. Martin—there might be heard kindred voices from the region's various storm-strong nations, people enduring against seemingly overwhelming odds, helping each other to bounce back in many unreported and underreported ways, kindred voices also from peoples and states of affected neighbors, Mexico, the USA …

The illustrations

The reproductions from the Maya codex or book in *Hurricane Protocol* are as much about catastrophe as they are in tribute to the languages and literatures of the Maya civilization and the *indígenas* of the Caribbean, from which the word hurricane derives.

Huracan—Huracán in Spanish; in Mayan languages Hunraqan ("one legged"), and often U K'ux Kaj ("Heart of Sky")—is a K'iche' Maya god of wind, storm, fire and one of the creator deities.

> "He also caused the Great Flood after the second generation of humans angered the gods. He supposedly lived in the windy mists above the floodwaters and repeatedly invoked 'earth' until land came up from the seas. ... The name may ultimately derive from huracan, a Carib word, and the source of the words hurricane and orcan (European windstorm)." (wikipedia.org)

The modernized drawings by Lacambalam that illustrate *Hurricane Protocol* are from pages 10 and 11 of the Maya codex at the museum of the Saxon

State and University Library Dresden, in Dresden, Germany. About 65% of the *Dresden Codex* contains "richly illustrated astronomical tables ... on eclipses, equinoxes and solstices," sidereal and synodic cycles. From sophisticated observations Mayans planned the calendar year, agriculture, and religious ceremonies. This oldest surviving "New World" book also includes multiplication tables and diagnoses of illnesses. (wikipedia.org/wiki/Maya_codices)

The *Dresden Codex* is the best preserved of only four hieroglyphic Maya codices thought to be in existence today. Thousands of the Maya books were destroyed by European priests and colonial officials during and after the genocidal invasion of the lands now known collectively as the Americas.

— Lasana M. Sekou
Rambaud, St. Martin

[1] A version of the "artist statement" and a selection of the "Hurricane Protocol poems" (9.8.17, 9.14.17, 9.18.17, 11.8.17, 11.16.17, 11.30.17), were first published in TRIPWIRE – *a journal of poetics* (14: 2018).

9.8.17

Hurricane Protocol

on the third day
we rise
again, from the ascension of dead pilings
throw'way from high and low places
pressing on, as we were
since the cut-ass of wind&wreckage

water water water for everyone please.

9.12.17
Hurricane Protocol

the wind-scald hillsides
gone to dusk
the mangroves, mauled, and things
that had brazen up and flush down to wetlands
float and sink
and currentless posts are lumbering well after
their lifeless veins, entangled alone and along
the roadside

dans la rue

in het steegje

à l'impasse

we are a world.unwired.

9.14.17
Hurricane Protocol

it may come to this
such an aftermath of time
of the nameless, hourlessfullonging days after
and a longing way
after what appears to be no end to a day
that you will see
roofless remains
of windowless panes
of unhinged doorlessness
of what was once upon a moment ago, known
as closed.belongings of unknown neighbors
now screen the leafless hillsides, broken
branches&bared roots
and all about us
a breaching silence enters the thresholds
breaching the cleavage,
the hallowed tender reach
the hollow you thought was fleshed full a'ready,
already baring to the brim

brimming with the family and friends
you had once upon a moment ago known
but now it's a breastbone pressed to open
a valley to rest bare belongings of the unknown

you see nothing
you hear nothing
you speak nothing
nothing in the repeating pings of it all
you smell nothing
you sense nothing
you will
nothing.

9.17.17

Hurricane Protocol

to recall
before the storm entered
the upper room
my eardrum housed a sound.
i would not be able to describe it now
but i'm sure it was a puff,
the heavy oak door butt my brow
and i would not be able to describe just how
but it had a purpose: certain and sudden so
my glasses fell out of sight,
i'm left on the landing, bareknuckle-
wringing the knob, hunched to a stiff bow,
THE_GODDAMN_KEEPER_OF_THE_FLAPPING_DOOR,
heat up to a fever from its fucking desire
to enter the slut of wilding wind, the raining
spiral of tearing glass
the roof timber lifting its wood to the zinc's
cutting remark
yet up to now

i could not tell you if it was a sound
that was sounding a consonance
to full the house with a sound
but the kind of symphony on the other side,
beseeching the door to beat off,
it did not wish us well

the two women dem
were calling out now
heading under the staircase
one protecting the elder,
who was already
without memory of this.

9.18.17
Hurricane Protocol

a stray debris of boys
tiefing gas
from the corral of cars
encamped in the deading night
crawling through frayed people's yard
sucking it out like a marrow to fill
their empty bikes, to motor their days to no end
it is in this short-
age time of everything that they prey&
pilfer. and this subject of absence
it becomes the object
of desire.

the stray dog
that had wagged its young self
right out of the same storm
plays all day long
with any and every one
and has fed into the yard's ownership,

it is in this short-
age time of everything, on these tiefing nights
he lays fast asleep.

9.19.17

Hurricane Protocol

the sky is brilliant
where the night colors itself deeply.
from a cement rooftop,
on the mounting road to *pic paradis*
we are pacing&dial-in to get outside
so certain self,
that out there is our world too&*tout moun* is
searching for us:
  lizette's husband is samuel
  freed's son is louis
  mel's father is on the roof steps
and everywhere is next door
  bev's by candlelight in the kitchen, calling nan
  nan's upstairs now, with alzheimer.
but the signal is without memory,
it refuses to come down to us
it has no history to leave the ground
the sweaty cell, from hand-to-hand,
seeks to imprison the ear

presses the temple
the eyes are lifted up
so sudden, the orison of grimaces gone
the horizon of our manacled events,
it has no cache for us.
the arc *seen.*
we are now free to roam . . .
  (the stray dog, he lays fast asleep
above us the cosmic black of beginnings
shepherds a tidal wave of stars
and if we can we can see,
we did not walk so good
since childhood.

9.22.17
Hurricane Protocol

"the sun crossed the line"
as today
so tonight
it is still
september.
fuck!

["The sun crossed the line," the term used in traditional St. Martin for the equinox in autumn, after which it was said that the hurricane period or season for the island was over. In 2017, the autumn date on which the sun crossed the celestial equator was September 22.]

10.31.17
Hurricane Protocol

as i turned, without a sound,
to see the confusion, the catastrophe,
the clearing on the path
the path became a voice too.
it turned into me.it spoke.

11.8.17
Hurricane Protocol

2017 | *the daily herald* reports: looting in st. martin.
1648 | *the treaty of concordia* records: looting of st. martin.

11.12.17
Hurricane Protocol

gale gusted winds
washed a way.
a whole circle of parents
    who long or enough watched the twilight
    wading in their plain sleep of pain or plenty
are walking away from our keep.
in visceral tides to year-one such times
    when greying tenants at the bedsides
    are tearing themselves away.
we are *the children* no more.

11.14.17

Hurricane Protocol

before it name irma there was grand case
there was rio grande
before it call maria there was barbuda
there was la habana,
ayay was there before
yabucoa was there, before
the road town and the valley,
lontan avan ou té vinn konnèt lapwent,
antes de punta cana,
and before the mayaimi too once,
there was huracan to name it
so that though it came first,
movingallovertheplace,
it had to have a name
to be known for what it is.

11.16.17

Hurricane Protocol

it was the pitch night ’n gale singing
a sweep of seawater fly ’cross the fishpond
bus’ open the house
lick ‘way the glass ’n the galvanize cut off,
a frigid wash up, all up
under the quarters ah meh bed
’n ’t push meh grown chil’ren back to meh
they groan, yes, ’n curl up)
  Faader, how i wish i could bear them back in
   meh now.
  how He hands mus’ be.full of it with this
   world, cold
trembling ’n, *oui*
tossing high on pondwater deep,
’n vie floating in air
wading cross-eyed as cackling rafters appear
  stark stares to the cracking shadows
  of crackling ceiling bones, splintering
  (wait!

let me think.what color was that sky again? …
wading…wading…holding on ’n wading
wading ’til morning come.like a water bag bus’!
neighbors deliver us down to ground.

one ah meh chil’ren dem
is still up there.

11.23.17
Hurricane Protocol

iiiiiiiiiiiiiiiiiiiiiir-
malonglongsong
ahlingehlongahsong
ahsirensingsingahgolonglong
song.

11.30.17
Hurricane Protocol

lead ben'

season en'

[A take on "Lead (metal) ben', story en'," which signals the end of a St. Martin folktale. St. Martin pronunciation: ben' = bend; en' = end. The Atlantic hurricane season ends November 30.]

BACK MATTER[S]

***Pero, niña,* we were children tho'**

(for s.c., who asked for a hurricane Irma rebuilding poem
but all that spiraled was this recall)

Remember when you had asked
if the soviet union would ever fall
?
and i said something like
so do all empires
with what must have been
the dumb frog smile of a know-it-all boy
and so you asked again, *how could that be*
?
with the incredulous forrid frown
of what i still swear is the oh so lovely girl
who had just refused the red hot iron
to press back her head ah hair
and i said, well, yes.

It was something about cycles in history
and that if there're people in it
to strap it on and ride

now, there lives the fight to the full
freedom, each time it comes up,
like precious doll orders that have yet to ship
with "the pilot standing by the helm and gazing
now at the full sails and now at the distance"[2]
is love's eternal threat,
the thread&thirst&thicket … for liberation.

[2] Gibran, Khalil, *The Prophet*.

Istanbul

Up to now
there is no man of clay
to fire his breath to breathe through
the nostrils of song
to fill this journey ...

Diyarbakır

7000 years on and all
you’ve lived to see the Gardens.
what happened?

Incroci a venezia

do not stagger from the spirit of names
you take
              or sense
                          or delude yourself as kindred
as you walk the way of these poets, beckoning
all along these shore lanes of water;
you will not be able to take your pale
to empty its sorrow
to drown it in marshlands
mined with the tidal breath
of not even a single craft-bearing muse
known to these:
                      byron
                                pound
                                          hemingway
                                walcott
                      lkj
              reed
these ones, mad men among them, their names
first to spiral at a salt reaper's crossings)

and come to find meena and tishani
who had themselves bared along here.

…

…

…

…

…

…

it is as if, among the coming and going ways
there are the wanderings; the waywards
those walking this way anyhow, well or weary
pilgrims on their journeying,
passing all along
these shore lanes of michela's lagoon,
city of water and islands.

to those to love&fight for

[from a dessalines of memories]

there are poets forbidden
from paradise
these types, tablets-breaking motherfuckers
they are marked as hell
the sayings they must do
the doings they must say
the memory manna they must carry away
way into themselves

and so that we can forgive,
they are bound to refuse
to wash out their mouths
to wash their mouths out, to take the bad rap,
slam it down&word up your "boom ba boom,"
<<launched from a baraka of tongues>>
they cannot even wash their hands of it all
the bloody stink&dirty business that they dig
unearth&hold^{up}&fling our way

barefoot from the sweep of shit they walking in
walking all the time
just a way at any point or way ahead of us
as if we asked them to be
scouts, or even one ah dem to be
the best street sweeper that ever lived.
coming&looking all kind of how but they are
all just poets
nothing more and
forbidden

these types, my beloved
cannot enter the promised land
with you.

holy tongue ah fire

from a call to the bar
on a respite night, at a hole in the wall
it ah come down just so
not to dis carnival
but to this underground space
where she call out: what about those parents
who beat
still
ah sick ah lick licks 'pon they oan chil'ren
to stop dem ah talk talk kwéyòl
all the patoispapiapisintakitakidemweahtalk?
an' t'day [head pointing@tonight's congregation]
the chil'ren dem in here happy happy
street sweepers.waitresses.mutes&addicts.
bartenders.strippers&hey, giol, wha' yu neem
y, dime, chulo, que lo que&wha' gwaan, son.
poets.prisonersbackout.bankers&big shit fakers
barbers&bakers&music hit makers.
gamblers.bundled bad&oi good, man.

maids.couriers.gypsies.all speaking
kwéyòllike sweet groan.people like unu who oan
language.
(but i'm just here, havin' a beer now)
her gurgle clamors hoarsely:
woi u ain sing 'bout dem so fo' kannaval
in those poem dem u wroitin'!?
(and here i am now, raisin' another beer)
there will be no carnival poem for those parents
this year.

bu’n, dump, bu’n

i see dung
(from mount william hill
(dusk tightens its color
(3 days&3 nights
a bed of fire.

DM continuum

Father son brother man
what would my life be but a blood-soaked street
stain of a visceral impasse,
the fire next time, the end
were it not for these.

riddim

tan tan

den den

yaya dem free

town

women

DNA

from motherland&old continents.
the flesh dealers cross tongues
licked raw the sweating skin
like t'was holy mead to steal
from the seething sear of greasy pain
of their branded captivessssssssssssssssssssssssssss

who is we
who waded blood seep in brine to know
what would come of this ?
who would put it to you,
that all who did eat this trade salt
marked and harvested in the excruciating cream
of your body's excreting pits
mined and dined from pyramid heaps,
raised on the banks of the great bay
that they did so eat of your body and blood ?

once 5000 captive saints trampled the crystals
crushed their seething sear of greasy pain]

lash and winged song rent the green hillside air
and the rhythm was a dance
that sent joy up in you, to wash yourself out
seasoning down whatever centuries became of it]
'n t'een yu 'lone,
bin a sing so sweet a'bi song dem so sad!
becausin wha', the enslavers also said&
wrote it down "in a book"
that the salt was sweet
the best EVER! but because, they say,
they ordered it so, reaped
in season, for the kingdoms of their time.

but who will put it to you now
old and new, if you missed the walk in
'long the path of ancestral crossings of
thorn feet ?
then from wherever&whenever you throd
to be.born here.to be.born to be here.to be we
to bear the saltpickers' code
you must wash yourself out
in the cradle of the nation

to be seasoned

to be all who claim&be/long&build&

love

the sweet s'maatin land.

Homework

(for rhoda and regina)

Who is to say
What is the useful vessel
Wherein the word just come
When ’t uttered so
Why ’t sweet to some
How ’t froighten others to death.

About the author

For over 40 years, the published poetry of St. Martin writer Lasana M. Sekou has been compared to the works of Oswald Mtshali, Kamau Brathwaite, Dylan Thomas, e.e. cummings, Aimé Césaire, and Linton Kwesi Johnson. However, to literary critic Howard Fergus in *Love Labor Liberation in Lasana Sekou*, "The voice that reaches us is *sui generis*, unique and Sekouesque." Sekou's poetry and fictions, *Nativity*, *The Salt Reaper*, *37 Poems*, *Love Songs Make You Cry*, and *Brotherhood of the Spurs* have been required reading at Caribbean, North American, and European universities. He is the editor of *National Symbols of St. Martin – A Primer* and producer of *Fête – The first recording of Traditional St. Martin festive music* by Tanny & The Boys. Sekou has presented papers and recited his poetry in the Caribbean, the Americas, Africa, Europe, and Asia. His poetry has been translated into Spanish, Dutch, French, German, Italian, Turkish, and Chinese. He is the co-founder of the St. Martin Book Fair, along with leading cultural activist Shujah Reiph. Awards and honors include the International Writers Workshop Visiting Fellow

(China), a James Michener Fellow (USA), a knighthood (the Netherlands), Recognition for literary excellence in the service of Caribbean unity (Dominican Republic), ACT Award Book of the Year, and the CTO Award of Excellence. In 2019, his short fiction collection *Brotherhood of the Spurs*, translated by Emilio Jorge Rodríguez as *Fraternidad de las Espuelas*, was published by Cuba's prestigious Editorial Arte y Literatura. Sekou is an advocate for the independence of St. Martin, a colony of France and the Netherlands.